Delish
CUPCAKES
by Color

Delish

CUPCAKES
by Color

More Than
100 Cupcakes
to Dazzle
and Amaze

HEARST BOOKS
New York

contents

introduction

Is there anyone who doesn't love cupcakes? These precious little offerings are just right for so many occasions, from children's birthday parties to formal receptions or to serve as individual celebration cakes for weddings, engagements and special events. *Delish Cupcakes by Color* is a book of ideas for the most gorgeous cupcakes in the world. We've divided the chapters by color: pink, white, yellow, blue/green and chocolate, but the beauty of this book is that you can adapt the decorations for these delightful little cakes and create any color combination you like. Our aim is to show you how to decorate more than 100 cupcakes in simple and pretty ways using store-bought chocolates, candies and decorations found in specialty candy shops, online, and in craft stores.

pink

jelly bean hearts

Top each cake generously with fluffy frosting. Cut an edge from one end of each small jelly bean, sandwich the cut ends together to make a heart shape. Position hearts on the cakes before the frosting has set.

dreamy rainbows

Color butter cream in varying shades of pinks and purples. Use small piping bags (without tips) to pipe bands of color on the top of each cake. Blend the colors slightly using a spatula.

roses & romance

Spread the top of each cake with a generous layer of white chocolate ganache. Top each cake with a store-bought dried rose bud.

sixlet-topped

Color butter cream pink. Spread the top of each cake generously with the butter cream. Top each cake with a red Sixlet.

chocolate truffle hearts

Color butter cream pale pink. Spread the top of each cake with butter cream. Fit a small piping bag with a small fluted tip, half-fill the bag with butter cream. Pipe a shell pattern around the edge of each cake. Top each cake with an iced heart-shaped chocolate truffle.

swirl of hearts

Color butter cream pink. Fit a large piping bag with a large star tip, half-fill the bag with butter cream. Pipe a large swirl of butter cream on top of each cake. Sprinkle butter cream with pink and red edible sugar hearts. Twist a length of gem strings on wire around each cake.

mosaic magic

Color butter cream pink. Spread the butter cream fairly thickly, but evenly, on the top of each cake. Decorate each cake in a mosaic pattern with pink candies–we used pink Skittles, pastilles, small candy pillows and sliced licorice cream rock logs. Fill in the gaps with pink dragées.

sour flowers

Color butter cream pink. Fit a large piping bag with a large star tip, half-fill the bag with the butter cream. Pipe small swirls of butter cream on the top of each cake. Split spearmint leaves in half horizontally, quarter strawberry-flavored sour straps lengthwise. Roll strips into spiral shapes, position on cakes with mint leaves. Position silver dragées in the center of the flowers.

coconut ice butterflies

Color glacé icing pink. Working with one cake at a time, spread the top of each cake with glacé icing, then immediately dip each in desiccated coconut. When the icing is set, cut a round hole, about ½ inch deep, in the top of each cake. Whip chilled heavy cream until it holds its shape. Halve the rounds of cake to make butterfly wings. Fill each hole with strawberry jam, then the cream. Position the wings on the cakes.

14

valentine hearts

Color a little fluffy frosting red. Half-fill a small piping bag (without a tip) with the red frosting. Spread white fluffy frosting on the top of each cake. Pipe three dots of the red frosting onto the unset white frosting. Pull a toothpick through each dot to make heart shapes.

hugs & kisses

Color butter cream pink. Spread the top of each cake evenly with the butter cream. Position sugar heart-shaped candies on cakes–in a cross for kisses and a circle for hugs.

berries & cream

Color unwhipped chilled heavy cream pale pink. Whip the cream until it barely holds its shape. Top each cake with cream and a mixture of your favorite berries–we used blueberries, raspberries and strawberries. Dust the berries with a little sifted powdered sugar.

hearts & arrows

Color butter cream red. Spread the top of each cake with the butter cream. Cut and trim chocolate-coated mint sticks to make arrows, position on cakes. Top cakes with red foil-covered chocolate hearts.

coconut cherry top

Fit a large piping bag with a large star tip, half-fill the bag with cream cheese frosting. Pipe a large swirl of the frosting on the top of each cake, sprinkle lightly with desiccated coconut, top with a maraschino cherry.

purple candies galore

Fit a large piping bag with a large star tip, half-fill the piping bag with fluffy mock cream. Pipe a large star on the top of each cake. Top cream with mounds of purple jelly candies–we used halved Jujubes, small jelly beans, Smarties and SweeTarts. Finish the cakes with purple candles.

sparkly baubles

Color butter cream pink. Fit a large piping bag with a large star tip, half-fill the piping bag with the butter cream. Pipe a generous swirl of butter cream on the top of each cake. Place edible lavender and white sugar baubles on butter cream.

pretty in purple

Spread the top of each cake evenly with butter cream. Working with one cake at a time, gently push a small (about ¾ inch long) leaf cutter into the butter cream, sprinkle some green sugar sprinkles inside the cutter, gently remove the cutter. Repeat this to make another leaf on the cake. Position purple edible sugar roses on cakes.

bunch of flowers

Spread the top of each cake evenly with butter cream. Make
the stems for the flowers by cutting thin strips (about 1½ inches
long) from green jelly worms. Tie a piece of ribbon around each
bunch of stems, position on cakes. Position pink and white
edible sugar flowers on cakes.

daisiness

Color butter cream pink. Spread the top of each cake fairly thickly, but evenly, with butter cream. Position about six white chocolate melts around the outside of each cake to make petals for the daisies, use pink jelly buttons (ours were anise in flavor) for the center of the daisies.

sequin swirl

Fit a large piping bag with a large star tip,
half-fill the bag with fluffy frosting. Pipe a large
swirl of the frosting on top of each cake. Sprinkle
cakes with edible sequins.

pink flowers

Fit a large piping bag with a large star tip, half-fill the bag with
fluffy mock cream. Pipe stars on the top of each cake. Cut white
marshmallows in half horizontally, dip the sticky side of each half
in pink sugar sprinkles, pinch one end of each half to make a petal
shape. Use five halves to make each flower, use some more sugar
sprinkles to fill in any white gaps on the marshmallows.

marbled magic

Color half a batch of fluffy mock cream pink. Gently mix the pink mock cream with the white cream to give a marbled effect. Fit a large piping bag with a large plain tip (or use the bag without a tip), half-fill the bag with the marbled cream. Pipe the cream into mounds on the top of each cake, decorate with pink and silver dragées. Top cakes with edible sugar flowers.

white

toasty coconut

Stir coarsely flaked coconut in a frying pan over a low heat until it is browned lightly; remove from the pan immediately to cool. Spread the top of each cake generously with cream cheese frosting; sprinkle with the toasted coconut.

mallow moments

Use scissors to cut toasted coconut-covered marshmallows into small pieces. Spread the top of each cake fairly thickly with butter cream; top with marshmallow pieces.

silver cloud

Fit a large piping bag with a large star tip, half-fill the bag with cream cheese frosting. Pipe a generous swirl of the frosting on the top of each cake, sprinkle with fine silver sprinkles. Top cakes with large silver dragées.

white choc curls

Use a sharp vegetable peeler to make chocolate curls by shaving the curls from the side of a bar of white chocolate. Spread the top of each cake generously with white chocolate ganache, top with the chocolate curls.

baby booties

Color cream cheese frosting white. Spread the frosting evenly over the top of each cake. Position edible sugar booties in the center of each cake, decorate with clusters of pink dragées.

baby rattle

Cut bamboo skewers into 2-inch lengths, secure three lengths together
with sticky tape to make handles for the rattles. Wrap pink and blue
ribbon around the handles to cover them; tie a bow around the top
of each handle. Push the handles into Ferrero Rocher white chocolate
truffles. Spread the top of each cake with whipped white chocolate
ganache, top with rattles.

wedding cakes aglow

Color butter cream white. Fit a large piping bag with a large star tip, half-fill the bag with butter cream. Pipe generous swirls on the tops of the cakes, sprinkle with silver cake sparkles. Push wedding cake candles into the stars.

rings forever

Spread the top of each cake evenly with fluffy frosting. Position silver dragées on each cake to make ring shapes, gently push the dragées into the frosting before it sets. We decided we'd like to have a pink diamond engagement ring, but we settled for pink dragées.

sugared violets

Brush a tiny amount of unbeaten egg white all over the petals
of freshly picked violets; sprinkle damp petals lightly with
superfine sugar, gently shake off any excess sugar. Dry the
violets on a thin wire rack. Spread the top of each cake quickly
with glacé icing. Position violets in the center of each cake.

rose petals

Spread the top of each cake with glacé icing. Position fresh rose petals in the center of each cake before the icing has set.

silver anniversary

Color butter cream white. Spread the top of each cake evenly with the butter cream. Position silver dragées on each cake to write 25, gently push the dragées into the butter cream.

pastel pink hearts

Brush the top of each cake with warmed strained apricot jam. Tint some ready-made fondant pink. Roll double the amount of fondant (to the amount of pink) between sheets of parchment paper until it is ⅛ inch thick. Roll the pink icing between sheets of parchment until ⅛ inch thick. Cut rounds of white icing large enough to cover the top of each cake (about 2½ inches). Use a 1-inch heart-shaped cutter to cut out hearts from the pink icing and from the center of the white icing rounds. Remove the white heart shapes, replace them with the pink hearts. Roll the icing again, gently, between sheets of parchment to ensure the hearts are in place. Position rounds on cakes.

sugared hearts

Use a hard plastic stencil that has varying sized and shaped hearts. Working with one cake at a time, place the stencil on the top of the cake, use a fine sifter to sift powdered sugar over the cut-out shapes. Gently lift the stencil off the cake. Brush the excess sugar from the stencil before using on the next cake.

daisy mints

Spread the top of each cake with fluffy frosting.
Use about six Tic Tacs to make the petals for
each daisy, push the Tic Tacs gently into the
frosting. Use tiny yellow flowers for the center
of the daisies.

snowflake sparkles

Melt some white chocolate melts. Half-fill a small piping bag (without a tip) with the melted chocolate. Pipe snowflake shapes onto parchment, top each with a large oval silver dragées; leave the snowflakes to set at room temperature. Spread the top of each cake with a thick layer of fluffy frosting and sprinkle cakes with sparkling pearl sugar crystals. Position a snowflake on each cake before the frosting has set.

sweet & simple

Working with one cake at a time, spread the top of each cake with glacé icing. Position a sugar flower in the center of each cake before the icing has set.

silver snowstorm

Dollop and swirl spoonfuls of fluffy frosting on the top of each cake. Sprinkle cakes with different sized silver dragées before the frosting has set.

dazzlers

Spread the top of each cake with glacé icing. Melt white chocolate melts, half-fill a small piping bag (without a tip) with the warm chocolate, quickly drizzle chocolate backwards and forwards over the set iced cakes. Quickly sprinkle cakes with small silver dragées before the chocolate has set.

purple power

Fit a large piping bag with a large star tip, half-fill the bag with fluffy frosting. Pipe a medium-sized star on top of each cake. Position a purple sugar flower in the center of each cake before the frosting has set.

fluffy frosted sprinkles

Fit a large piping bag with a large star tip, half-fill the bag with fluffy frosting. Pipe a generous swirl of frosting on the top of each cake. Sprinkle each cake with bright colored sprinkles before the frosting has set.

butterflies

Whip chilled heavy cream until it barely holds its shape. Cut a round hole, about 1 inch deep, in the top of each cake. Halve the rounds of cake to make butterfly wings. Fill each hole with strawberry jam, then the cream. Position the wings on the cakes. Dust cakes lightly with sifted powdered sugar.

snowflakes

Dollop the top of each cake with a generous spoonful of fluffy frosting. Use
a spatula to shape and swirl the "snow", sprinkle cakes with edible sugar
snowflakes.

yellow

checkerboard

Color butter cream white. Spread the top of each cake evenly with the butter cream. Remove orange fondant sections from Licorice Allsorts, cut each section into four squares. Make a checkerboard pattern on the cakes with the fondant squares.

dotty

Color butter cream orange. Spread the top of each cake evenly with the butter cream. Position orange Smarties and orange mini M&M's on each cake.

fruity stripes

Spread the top of each cake evenly with butter cream. Halve yellow and orange soft fruit sticks crossways. Trim the ends of the fruit sticks to fit neatly on the top of each cake.

spirals

Color butter cream yellow. Spread the top of each cake evenly with the butter cream. Make spirals, starting from the center of the cake, using different sized yellow candies– we used Rainbow Chips, then mini M&M's, then Smarties to create the spiral.

fruity citrus cakes

Half-fill a large piping bag (without a tip) with fluffy frosting. Pipe swirls of the frosting on top of each cake. Position orange and yellow jelly fruit slices on the frosting before it has set.

banana split

Fit a large piping bag with a large star tip, half-fill the bag with butter cream. Pipe a swirl of butter cream on the top of each cake. Top cakes with small white mini marshmallows and banana candies. Drizzle melted dark chocolate over the top of each cake, sprinkle with chocolate sprinkles.

ring of roses

Spread the top of each cake with butter cream. Position a circle of yellow and/or white sugar roses in the center of each cake.

baby feet

Color butter cream white. Spread the top of each cake evenly with the butter cream. Split small yellow jelly beans in half lengthwise, position on cakes. Use yellow writing icing to pipe toes.

button-ups

Brush the top of each cake with a little warmed strained jam. Tint some ready-made fondant yellow. Roll pieces of the icing between sheets of parchment to about ⅛ inch thick. Cut rounds from the icing large enough to cover the top of each cake (about 2½ inches). Position the rounds on each cake. Use the blunt edge of a slightly smaller round cutter to mark the edge of the buttons. Make button holes from mini mints.

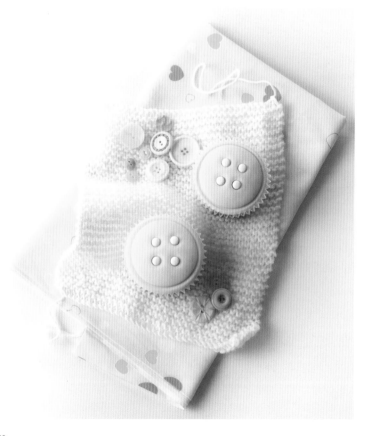

gift boxes

Color butter cream yellow. Spread the top of each cake generously with the butter cream. Tie ribbon around Licorice Allsorts to make gifts. Position gift boxes in the center of each cake.

baby carrot cakes

Fit a large piping bag with a large star tip, half-fill the bag with cream cheese frosting. Pipe a swirl of the frosting on the top of each cake. Sprinkle cakes with orange sprinkles, top with tiny edible sugar carrots.

lemon curd creams

Cut deep triangular holes into the top of each cake; reserve lids. Whip heavy cream until it holds its shape. Fit a large piping bag with a large star tip, half-fill the bag with the cream. Fill the holes with lemon curd. Pipe cream over the curd, drizzle with a little extra curd. Position lids in the center of each cake. Dust cakes with a little sifted powdered sugar.

gold star

Brush the top of each cake with warmed strained apricot jam. Knead equal quantities of white and chocolate ready-made fondant together to make a milk-chocolate-colored icing. Roll the icing between sheets of parchment to ⅓ inch thick. Cut rounds from the icing large enough to cover the top of each cake (about 2½ inches). Cut a 2-inch star shape from the center of each round. Position the rounds on top of each cake. Fill the star shapes with a single layer of gold dragées.

dainties

Spread the top of each cake generously with butter cream. Remove green fondant sections from Licorice Allsorts. Cut out leaf shapes from the fondant, using either a ¾-inch leaf cutter or a sharp pointed vegetable knife. Top each cake with a leaf and an edible sugar flower.

mellow yellow

Fit a large piping bag with a large star tip,
half-fill the bag with butter cream. Pipe a large
swirl on the top of each cake, sprinkle with
yellow sprinkles.

sunflower

Spread the top of each cake with
a thick layer of butter cream.
Position a row of candy corn
around the outside edge of each
cake, then position another row of
the corn on the inside. Sprinkle
some yellow sugar crystals in the
center of each cake.

stardust

Fit a large piping bag with a large star tip, half-fill the bag with butter cream. Pipe a large star on the top of each cake. Remove the orange and yellow fondant sections from Licorice Allsorts. Use a miniature star cutter to cut out stars and position them on the butter cream.

banana & passionfruit cream

Dollop generous spoonfuls of whipped cream on the top of each cake. Place finely-sliced banana on top of the cream then drizzle with passionfruit pulp.

spotty

Tint ready-made white fondant yellow. Roll an equal quantity of white fondant (to the yellow) between sheets of parchment until it is ⅛ inch thick. Roll the yellow icing between sheets of parchment until it is ⅛ inch thick. Cut ¾-inch rounds, very close together, from both pieces of icing. Place white rounds in the holes left in the yellow icing, and the yellow rounds in the holes left in the white icing. Roll both pieces of icing again, between sheets of parchment, to make sure the rounds are in place. Brush the top of each cake with a little strained warm apricot jam. Cut rounds from each piece of icing large enough to cover the top of each cake (about 2½ inches). Position rounds on each cake.

daisy glaze

Working with one cake at a time, spread the top
of each cake with lemon glacé icing. Position
edible sugar flowers in the center of each before
the icing has set.

blue & green

minty snowflakes

Color butter cream blue. Spread the top of each cake evenly with the butter cream. Gently push mini mints into the butter cream in the shape of snowflakes. Dust cakes with sifted powdered sugar.

christmas baubles

Color butter cream blue. Spread the top of each cake evenly with the butter cream. Outline the pattern for the baubles and the loop with blue dragées. Use edible blue glitter to fill in the pattern. Make a loop with a thin strip of licorice lace, gently push the loop into the butter cream and top with a white marshmallow.

christmas berries

Color butter cream white. Spread the top of each cake with the butter cream. Split spearmint leaf jellies in half horizontally, gently push the leaves into the butter cream. Use red Sixlets to make the berries.

christmas wreaths

Color butter cream white. Spread the top of each cake with a thick layer of the butter cream. Split spearmint leaf jellies in half horizontally, you'll need about six leaves for each cake. Gently push the halved leaves, smooth-side up and slightly overlapping, into butter cream in the shape of a wreath. Decorate leaves with silver and gold dragées.

blueberries & cream

Top each cake with generous spoonfuls of sweetened whipped cream.
Place fresh blueberries on the cream. Dust cakes with finely sifted
powdered sugar.

sugared almonds

Spread the top of each cake with glacé icing. Position a blue sugared almond in the center of each cake before the icing has set.

blue heaven

Spread the top of each cake with butter cream. Position four or five edible blue sugar flowers on the top of each cake.

starbright

Tint ready-made fondant blue. Roll an equal quantity of white fondant (to the blue) between sheets of parchment until it is ⅛ inch thick. Roll blue icing between sheets of parchment until it is ⅛ inch thick. Use a 1-inch star cutter to cut out star shapes, very close together, from both pieces of icing. Place white stars in the holes left in the blue icing. (If you like, you can also place some of the blue stars in the holes left in the white icing–we used just the white stars.) Roll icing again, between sheets of parchment, to ensure the stars are in place. Brush the top of each cake with a little strained warmed apricot jam. Cut rounds from icing large enough to cover the top of each cake (about 2½ inches). Position rounds on each cake.

on top of the hill

Color butter cream green. Color desiccated coconut green by rubbing coloring into the coconut. Dollop a generous amount of butter cream on the top of each cake and shape into mounds; sprinkle with green coconut. Melt milk chocolate melts, half-fill a small piping bag (without a tip) with the chocolate. Pipe 40 (or whatever numbers you prefer) onto a piece of parchment, leave the numbers to set at room temperature. Push the numbers gently into the side of each butter cream mound.

peppermint cream sundae

Color butter cream green, then flavor the cream with a little peppermint oil or extract. Break up some Chick-O-Sticks, and stir through the butter cream. Dollop a generous amount of butter cream on the top of each cake then use a spatula to form a scoop of ice-cream. Spread some melted, cooled milk chocolate over the butter cream, then sprinkle with more crumbled Chick-O-Sticks before the chocolate has set.

three of hearts

Color fluffy frosting green. Use a ¾-inch heart cutter to cut out heart shapes from Mint Patties. Spread the top of each cake fairly thickly with the frosting. Position three hearts on each cake before the frosting has set.

mosaic magic

Spread the top of each cake fairly thickly with white chocolate ganache. Decorate each cake in a mosaic pattern with blue and green candies—we used Lifesavers, mini M&M's, Skittles and baby jelly beans. Gently push the candy into the ganache.

make a wish

Split white mini marshmallows in half
horizontally. Color glacé icing blue.
Working with one cake at a time, spread
the top of each cake evenly with the glacé
icing. Position five mini marshmallow
halves for petals and a blue dragée in the
center, before the icing has set. Half-fill a
small piping bag (without a tip) with royal
icing, pipe the stems on the cakes after
the icing has set.

glamour masks

Color butter cream blue. Spread the top of each cake evenly with the butter cream. Make a mask shape on each cake using silver and blue dragées in a single layer. Push each dragée gently into the butter cream. Use sticks cut from lollipops for the handles of the masks. Use small pieces of ribbon and sugar flowers to cover and decorate the top of the handles.

blue crystals

Fit a large piping bag with a star tip, half-fill the bag with butter cream.
Pipe large swirls of butter cream on the top of each cake, sprinkle with
blue sugar crystals.

cute as a button

Color butter cream white. Spread the top of each cake with the butter cream. Gently push six small green pillow candies into the top of each cake to make a flower shape. Place a brown Smartie in the center of each flower.

chocolate

chocolate kisses

Whip white chocolate ganache until fluffy. Spread the top of each cake with ganache. Position milk chocolate kisses and small chocolate star sprinkles over cakes.

rainbows

Fit a large piping bag with a large star tip, half-fill the bag with dark chocolate ganache. Pipe generous swirls on the top of each cake. Decorate cakes with multi-colored Smarties and Rainbow Chips.

peanut heaven

Marble some chunky peanut butter through milk chocolate ganache. Fit a large piping bag with a large star tip, half-fill the bag with the ganache mixture. Pipe generous swirls of the ganache on the top of each cake, sprinkle with crushed peanut brittle.

malt ganache

Fit a large piping bag with a large star tip, half-fill the bag with whipped milk chocolate ganache. Pipe generous swirls on the top of each cake. Decorate cakes with malt balls, brown mini M&M's, gold dragées and gold edible glitter.

fairy coconut cakes

Working with one cake at a time, dip the top of each cake in chocolate glacé icing, then immediately dip in desiccated coconut. When the icing has set, cut a 1½-inch-wide hole, about ½ inch deep, in the top of each cake. Fill each hole with whipped cream. Place the rounds on each cake.

marbled choc caramel

Spread the top of each cake with a fairly thick layer of dark chocolate ganache. Dollop about six small dots of caramel sauce on the ganache. Pull a skewer back and forth through the caramel for a marbled effect.

dragonfly

Spread the top of each
cake with a thick layer
of chocolate butter cream.
Make the dragonfly
bodies using about four
white chocolate chips
each. Cut chocolate
nonpareils into quarters,
position two quarters
on each cake for wings.
Use pieces of shredded
coconut for antennae.

mochaflies

Spread the top of each cake evenly with mocha butter cream. Cut thin strips, about 1½ inches long, from licorice strips, position on cakes to make bodies and antennae of mochaflies. Cut milk- and dark-chocolate-coated coffee beans in half crosswise, position, cut-side up, for wings.

imelda

Spread the top of each cake with white chocolate ganache. Attach small edible sugar butterflies to chocolate high-heeled shoes with tiny dabs of ganache. Position shoes on cakes.

chocky lips

Dollop top of each cake with milk chocolate ganache, sprinkle with red cake sparkles. Top each cake with a pair of red jelly lips.

milkyway stars

Spread the top of each cake with a thick layer of dark chocolate ganache. Position milk chocolate stars on cakes.

magical mushrooms

Spread the top of each cake with a thick layer of dark chocolate ganache.
Position white chocolate melts and white chocolate chips on cakes.

music music

Melt some white chocolate melts. Half-fill a small piping bag (without a tip) with the chocolate. Pipe treble clefs and musical notes onto a parchment-lined tray; set at room temperature. Spread the top of each cake with a generous layer of milk chocolate ganache. Cut thin strips from licorice strips, position the strips on each cake to make staves. Secure treble clefs and notes on the staves with tiny dabs of ganache.

chocolate hearts

Dollop the top of each cake with generous spoonfuls of whipped milk chocolate ganache. Remove foil wrappers from chocolate hearts, gently push a heart into the ganache. Dust cakes with sifted cocoa powder.

marshmallow snowballs

Spread the top of each cake with an even layer of dark chocolate ganache. Position a coconut and chocolate-coated Eskimo Snowball on the cakes.

choc mint crush

Spread the top of each cake generously with dark chocolate ganache. Top each cake with crushed mint chocolate candies.

chocolate easter eggs

Spread the top of each cake with whipped white chocolate ganache.
Position small chocolate easter eggs in the center of each cake.

cakeuccinos

Spread the top of each cake evenly with fluffy mock cream. Working with one cake at a time, hold a cappuccino stencil closely to the top of the cake. Use a fine sifter to sift cocoa powder over the cutout shape. Gently lift the stencil away from the cake. Brush the excess cocoa from the stencil before using on the next cake.

cross your heart

Spread the top of each cake evenly with dark chocolate ganache. Melt some white chocolate melts. Half-fill a small piping bag (without a tip) with the chocolate. Working with one cake at a time, pipe random criss-cross lines of chocolate across the cake. Position red sugar hearts on chocolate before it has set.

nest egg

Spread the top of each cake with a thick layer of dark chocolate ganache. Break Chick-O-Sticks into pieces, push the pieces gently into the ganache to make nests. Position blue sugared almonds in the center of each nest.

graduation

Spread the top of each cake with white chocolate ganache. Place a Junior Mint in the center of each cake, position a square of chocolate on the mint ball to make a mortarboard. Cut thin strips, about 1½ inches long, from licorice strips, split the end of each strip into fine strips to make tassels. Attach a tassel to each mortarboard with a tiny dab of melted dark chocolate.

milk chocolate whip

Fit a large piping bag with a large piping tip, half-fill the bag with whipped chocolate ganache. Pipe large swirls of the ganache on the top of each cake. Sprinkle with chocolate sprinkles.

cakes

Here's a selection of some of our favorite cupcake-friendly recipes. There's a rich but easy fruit cake, old favorites like banana, carrot and butter cakes, a great quick-mix chocolate cake, a light-as-a-feather sponge cake and a good selection of cakes for people who have various allergies. Each hole in the standard muffin pan we used had a fluid capacity of ⅓ cup. The paper cases we used had a side measurement of 1½ inches and a base diameter of 1¾ inches.

vanilla butter cakes

1 cup self-rising flour
6 tablespoons softened butter
1 teaspoon vanilla extract
½ cup superfine sugar
2 eggs
2 tablespoons milk

1 Preheat oven to 375°F/350°F fan-forced. Line eight holes of 12-hole muffin pan with paper cases.
2 Sift flour into small bowl, add butter, extract, sugar, eggs and milk; beat with electric mixer on low speed until ingredients are combined. Increase speed to medium; beat until mixture is changed to a paler color.
3 Drop ¼ cup of mixture into cases. Bake about 20 minutes. Stand cakes 5 minutes before turning top-side up onto wire rack to cool.
Makes 8

sponge cakes

3 eggs
½ cup superfine sugar
¼ cup corn starch
¼ cup all-purpose flour
¼ cup self-rising flour

1 Preheat oven to 375°F/350°F fan-forced. Line ten holes of 12-hole muffin pan with paper cases.
2 Beat eggs in small bowl with electric mixer about 5 minutes or until thick and creamy; gradually add sugar, one tablespoon at a time, beating until sugar dissolves between additions. Transfer to large bowl.
3 Meanwhile, sift the dry ingredients twice, then sift over egg mixture; fold ingredients together.
4 Drop ¼ cup of mixture into cases. Bake about 25 minutes. Turn cakes immediately onto wire rack, then turn top-side up to cool.
Makes 10

quick-mix chocolate cakes

1 cup self-rising flour
½ cup all-purpose flour
⅓ cup cocoa powder
¾ cup superfine sugar
14 tablespoons softened butter
3 eggs
½ cup milk

1 Preheat oven to 375°F/350°F
fan-forced. Line 15 holes of
two 12-hole muffin pans with paper
cases.
2 Sift dry ingredients into medium
large bowl, add remaining
ingredients; beat with electric mixer
on low speed until ingredients
are combined. Increase speed to
medium; beat until mixture
is smooth and has changed
to a paler color.
3 Drop ¼ cup of mixture into
cases. Bake about 20 minutes.
Stand cakes 5 minutes before
turning top-side up onto wire rack
to cool.
Makes 15

dark chocolate mud cakes

2 ounces bittersweet chocolate,
    chopped coarsely
⅔ cup water
6 tablespoons softened butter
1 cup firmly packed brown
    sugar
2 eggs
⅔ cup self-rising flour
2 tablespoons cocoa powder
⅓ cup almond meal

1 Preheat oven to 350°F/325°F
fan-forced. Line 12-hole muffin pan
with paper cases.
2 Stir chocolate and the water in
small saucepan over low heat until
smooth.
3 Beat butter, sugar and eggs
in small bowl with electric mixer
until light and fluffy. Stir in sifted
flour and cocoa, meal and warm
chocolate mixture.
4 Drop ¼ cup of mixture into
cases. Bake about 25 minutes.
Stand cakes 5 minutes before
turning top-side up onto wire rack
to cool.
Makes 12

caramel mud cakes

1 stick butter, chopped coarsely

3½ ounces white chocolate, chopped coarsely

⅔ cup firmly packed brown sugar

¼ cup golden syrup

⅔ cup milk

1 cup all-purpose flour

⅓ cup self-rising flour

1 egg

1 Preheat oven to 350°F/325°F fan-forced. Line 12-hole muffin pan with paper cases.
2 Stir the butter, chocolate, sugar, syrup and milk in small saucepan over low heat until smooth. Transfer mixture to medium bowl; cool 15 minutes.
3 Whisk sifted flours into chocolate mixture, then egg.
4 Drop ¼ cup of mixture into cases. Bake about 30 minutes. Stand cakes 5 minutes before turning top-side up onto wire rack to cool.
Makes 12

white chocolate mud cakes

1 stick butter, chopped coarsely

2½ ounces white chocolate, chopped coarsely

1 cup superfine sugar

½ cup milk

½ cup all-purpose flour

½ cup self-rising flour

1 egg

1 Preheat oven to 350°F/325°F fan-forced. Line 12-hole muffin pan with paper cases.
2 Stir butter, chocolate, sugar and milk in small saucepan over low heat until smooth. Transfer mixture to medium bowl; cool 15 minutes.
3 Whisk sifted flours into chocolate mixture, then egg.
4 Drop ¼ cup of mixture into cases. Bake about 30 minutes. Stand cakes 5 minutes before turning top-side up onto wire rack to cool.
Makes 12

rich fruit cakes

6 tablespoons softened butter

**½ cup firmly packed
brown sugar**

2 eggs

**1 tablespoon orange
marmalade**

**2⅓ cups mixed dried fruit,
chopped finely**

⅔ cup all-purpose flour

2 tablespoons self-rising flour

1 teaspoon pie spice

2 tablespoons sweet sherry

**1 tablespoon sweet sherry,
extra**

1 Preheat oven to 325°F/300°F
fan-forced. Line eight holes
of 12-hole muffin pan with
paper cases.
2 Beat butter, sugar and eggs
in small bowl with electric mixer
until combined; transfer mixture to
medium bowl. Stir in marmalade
and fruit.
3 Stir in sifted dry ingredients and
sherry.
4 Drop ⅓ cup of mixture into
cases. Bake about 1¼ hours. Brush
cakes with extra sherry. Cover pan
with foil; cool cakes in pan.
Makes 8

banana cakes

1 stick softened butter

**¾ cup firmly packed
brown sugar**

2 eggs

1½ cups self-rising flour

½ teaspoon baking soda

1 teaspoon pie spice

1 cup mashed overripe banana

½ cup sour cream

¼ cup milk

1 Preheat oven to 375°F/350°F
fan-forced. Line 16 holes of
two 12-hole muffin pans with
paper cases.
2 Beat butter and sugar in small
bowl with electric mixer until light
and fluffy. Beat in eggs, one at a
time.
3 Transfer mixture to large bowl;
stir in sifted dry ingredients,
banana, sour cream and milk,
in two batches.
4 Drop ¼ cup of mixture into
cases. Bake about 30 minutes.
Stand cakes 5 minutes before
turning top-side up onto wire rack
to cool.
Makes 16

carrot cakes

1 cup vegetable oil

1⅓ cups firmly packed
  brown sugar

3 eggs

3 cups firmly packed,
  coarsely grated carrot

1 cup coarsely chopped walnuts

2½ cups self-rising flour

½ teaspoon baking soda

2 teaspoons pie spice

1 Preheat oven to 375°F/350°F
fan-forced. Line 18 holes of
two 12-hole muffin pans with
paper cases.
2 Beat oil, sugar and eggs in small
bowl with electric mixer until thick.
Transfer mixture to large bowl;
stir in carrot, nuts, then sifted dry
ingredients.
3 Drop ¼ cup of mixture into
cases. Bake about 30 minutes.
Stand cakes 5 minutes before
turning top-side up onto wire rack
to cool.
Makes 18

lemon poppy seed cakes

⅓ cup poppy seeds

¼ cup milk

12 tablespoons softened butter

2 teaspoons finely grated
  lemon rind

1 cup superfine sugar

3 eggs

1½ cups self-rising flour

½ cup all-purpose flour

½ cup almond meal

½ cup orange juice

1 Preheat oven to 375°F/350°F
fan-forced. Line 12-hole muffin pan
with paper cases.
2 Combine seeds and milk in small
bowl, stand 20 minutes.
3 Beat butter, rind and sugar in
small bowl with electric mixer until
fluffy; beat in eggs one at a time.
Transfer mixture to medium bowl;
stir in sifted flours, meal, juice and
milk mixture, in two batches.
4 Drop ⅓ cup of mixture into
cases. Bake about 35 minutes.
Stand cakes 5 minutes before
turning top-side up onto wire rack
to cool.
Makes 12

marble cakes

1 stick softened butter
1 teaspoon vanilla extract
⅔ cup superfine sugar
2 eggs
1¼ cups self-rising flour
⅓ cup milk
pink food coloring
1 tablespoon cocoa powder
2 teaspoons milk, extra

1 Preheat oven to 375°F/350°F fan-forced. Line 12-hole muffin pan with paper cases.
2 Beat the butter, extract, sugar and eggs in small bowl with electric mixer until fluffy. Stir in sifted flour and milk in two batches.
3 Divide mixture among three small bowls. Tint one mixture pink. Blend sifted cocoa with extra milk in cup; stir into the second bowl of mixture. Leave the third bowl of mixture plain.
4 Drop alternate spoonfuls of mixtures into cases. Pull a skewer through mixtures for a marbled effect. Bake about 20 minutes. Stand cakes for 5 minutes before turning top-side up onto wire rack to cool.
Makes 12

ginger buttermilk cakes

½ cup firmly packed brown sugar
½ cup all-purpose flour
½ cup self-rising flour
¼ teaspoon baking soda
1 teaspoon ground ginger
½ teaspoon ground cinnamon
¼ teaspoon ground nutmeg
6 tablespoons softened butter
1 egg
¼ cup buttermilk
2 tablespoons golden syrup

1 Preheat oven to 350°F/325°F fan-forced. Line nine holes of 12-hole muffin pan with paper cases.
2 Sift dry ingredients into small bowl; add remaining ingredients. Beat mixture with electric mixer on low speed until ingredients are combined. Increase speed to medium; beat until mixture is changed to a paler color.
3 Drop ¼ cup of mixture into cases. Bake about 35 minutes. Stand cakes 5 minutes before turning top-side up onto wire rack to cool.
Makes 9

flourless choc hazelnut cakes

¼ cup cocoa powder

¼ cup hot water

3½ ounces bittersweet
  chocolate, melted

7 tablespoons butter, melted

1 cup firmly packed
  brown sugar

¾ cup hazelnut meal

3 eggs, separated

1 Preheat oven to 375°F/350°F
fan-forced. Line nine holes
of 12-hole muffin pan with
paper cases.
2 Blend cocoa with the water
in medium bowl until smooth. Stir
in chocolate, butter, sugar, meal
and egg yolks.
3 Beat egg whites in small bowl
with electric mixer until soft peaks
form; fold into chocolate mixture in
two batches.
4 Pour ⅓ cup of mixture into
cases. Bake 1 hour 10 minutes.
Stand cakes 5 minutes before
turning top-side up onto wire rack
to cool.
Makes 9

chocolate cakes

½ cup dairy-free spread

3½ ounces bittersweet
  chocolate (70% cocoa solids),
  chopped coarsely

¾ cup soy milk

¾ cup superfine sugar

1 cup self-rising flour

½ cup all-purpose flour

2 tablespoons cocoa powder

1 Preheat oven to 325°F/300°F fan-
forced. Line 12-hole muffin pan with
paper cases.
2 Combine spread, chocolate, milk
and sugar in medium saucepan; stir
over low heat until smooth. Transfer
mixture to large bowl; cool 10
minutes. Whisk in sifted flours and
cocoa until smooth.
3 Pour ¼ cup of mixture into cases.
Bake about 25 minutes. Stand
cakes 5 minutes before turning top-
side up onto wire rack to cool.
Makes 12

gluten-free mandarin cakes

4 small mandarins
2 cups macadamias
2 sticks softened butter
1 cup superfine sugar
3 eggs
1 cup polenta
1 teaspoon gluten-free
baking powder

1 Cover whole mandarins in medium saucepan with cold water; bring to a boil. Drain; repeat process twice. Cool.
2 Preheat oven to 375°F/350°F fan-forced. Line 18 holes of two 12-hole muffin pans with paper cases.
3 Blend or process nuts finely.
4 Halve mandarins; discard the seeds. Blend mandarins until pulpy.
5 Beat butter and sugar in small bowl with electric mixer until light and fluffy. Beat in eggs, one at a time. Transfer mixture to large bowl; stir in polenta, baking powder, nuts and mandarin.
6 Drop ¼ cup of mixture into cases. Bake about 25 minutes. Stand cakes 5 minutes before turning, top-side up, onto wire rack to cool.
Makes 18

gluten-free butter cakes

14 tablespoons softened butter
2¼ cups gluten-free
self-rising flour
1 cup superfine sugar
½ cup milk
2 eggs
2 egg whites

1 Preheat oven to 375°F/350°F fan-forced. Line two 12-hole muffin pans with paper cases.
2 Beat butter in medium bowl with electric mixer until it changes to a paler color.
3 Meanwhile, sift the flour with ¼ cup of the sugar, beat flour mixture and milk into butter, in two batches, until combined.
4 Beat eggs and egg whites in small bowl with electric mixer until thick and creamy. Gradually add remaining sugar, beating until dissolved between additions. Gradually beat egg mixture into flour mixture on a low speed.
5 Drop 2½ level tablespoons of mixture into cases. Bake about 20 minutes. Stand cakes 5 minutes before turning top-side up onto wire rack to cool.
Makes 24

frostings & finishes

All of the cupcakes in this book have a topping of some sort, from the simplest glaze to a lavish ganache. It's up to you to decide on the number of the cupcakes to make, and the type and amount of frosting you need to finish the cakes. Here are all the icings, frostings, etc., we've chosen to use in this book, but let your imagination loose and do your own thing with different cake and frosting combinations. There are variations within the recipes to broaden your choices. In butter-based recipes, such as Butter Cream and Fluffy Mock Cream, we prefer to use unsalted butter–there is a little difference in the taste. Make sure you have the butter at room temperature, not melted or too hard; it's important to beat the butter until it is as white as possible for the best results. You can buy white coloring from cake decorator's suppliers if you need to whiten a butter-based icing. Powdered sugar is best for royal icing and makes a good glaze for cakes. Store-bought fondant is a great product and easy to use. Use colorings sparingly at first until you determine their strength.

butter cream

Add any flavored oil or extract you like to butter cream. Beat it in with the butter for the best flavor. Any citrus rind can be used. Beat 2 teaspoons finely grated rind with the butter and use the corresponding juice instead of the milk. Butter cream is the most popular type of frosting, it's easy to spread and handle. Be aware that it's cream in color, so any added coloring will pick up a yellow tinge, particularly pinks and reds.

1 stick butter, softened
1½ cups powdered sugar
2 tablespoons milk

1 Beat butter in small bowl with electric mixer until as white as possible; beat in sifted sugar and milk, in two batches.
Makes 1¾ cups

variations
chocolate Sift 2 tablespoons cocoa powder with the sugar.
mocha Warm 1 tablespoon of the milk, stir in 2 teaspoons instant coffee granules, add the remaining tablespoon of milk. Sift 2 tablespoons of cocoa powder with the sugar.

ganache

Ganache can be made with milk, dark or white good-quality chocolate. The methods are the same, but the amount of chocolate varies slightly, as do the resulting quantities. Ganache can be used while still warm and pourable, or it can be beaten with a wooden spoon until spreadable. If you want the ganache lighter and fluffier–referred to as whipped ganache–beat the cooled mixture in a small bowl with an electric mixer.

milk chocolate
½ cup cream
7 ounces milk chocolate, chopped coarsely
Makes 1 cup

dark chocolate
½ cup cream
7 ounces bittersweet chocolate, chopped coarsely
Makes 1 cup

white chocolate
½ cup cream
12½ ounces white chocolate, chopped coarsely
Makes 1½ cups

1 Bring cream to a boil in a small saucepan; remove from heat. When bubbles subside, add chocolate; stir until smooth.

glacé icing

Quick and easy, glacé icing is worth learning to make properly. You can alter the flavor, texture and color easily. The butter (you can use vegetable oil instead) keeps the icing slightly soft, so it cuts well. Without the butter or oil, the icing tends to shatter. It's important that the icing is only warm, not hot, while it's being stirred over the pan of water–it will crystallize if over-heated.

2 cups powdered sugar
1 teaspoon butter
2 tablespoons hot water,
  approximately

1 Sift sugar into small heatproof bowl; stir in butter and enough of the hot water to make a thick paste. Place bowl over small saucepan of simmering water; stir until icing is spreadable.
Makes 1 cup

variations

chocolate Sift 2 teaspoons cocoa powder with the sugar.
coffee Dissolve 1 teaspoon instant coffee granules in the water.
mocha Sift 2 teaspoons cocoa powder with the icing sugar, and dissolve 1 teaspoon instant coffee granules in the hot water.
passionfruit Stir 1 tablespoon passionfruit pulp into mixture.

royal icing

Royal icing begins to set as soon as it's exposed to the air, so keep the icing covered tightly with plastic wrap while you're not working with it. Once the icing has dried, it will set hard, and when it's cut, it will shatter. But, it's great for piping, coloring, spreading and making snowy mounds.

1½ cups powdered sugar
1 egg white
½ teaspoon lemon juice

1 Sift sugar through a very fine sieve. Lightly beat egg white in small bowl with an electric mixer; add sugar, a tablespoon at a time. When icing reaches firm peaks, use a wooden spoon to beat in juice; cover tightly with plastic wrap.
Makes 1 cup

cream cheese frosting

For a citrus flavor, beat 2 teaspoons finely grated orange, lemon or lime rind with the butter and cream cheese. This frosting goes particularly well with carrot and banana cakes. Like butter cream, it is very user-friendly, but takes colorings slightly better than butter cream.

2 tablespoons butter, softened
3 ounces cream cheese, softened
1½ cups powdered sugar

1 Beat butter and cheese in small bowl with electric mixer until light and fluffy; gradually beat in sifted powdered sugar.
Makes 1¼ cups

fluffy frosting

If you don't have a candy thermometer, boil the syrup until it's thick with heavy bubbles. Remove from heat, let bubbles subside, then reassess the thickness of the syrup. Once the frosting is made, you can spread it for quite a while before it begins to set and lose its gloss, developing a meringue-like crust. It's perfect for coloring and piping.

1 cup superfine sugar
⅓ cup water
2 egg whites

1 Combine sugar and the water in small saucepan; stir over heat, without boiling, until sugar is dissolved. Boil, uncovered, without stirring, about 5 minutes or until syrup reaches 240°F on a candy thermometer. Syrup should be thick but not colored. Remove from heat, allow bubbles to subside.
2 Beat egg whites in small bowl with electric mixer until soft peaks form. While motor is running, add hot syrup in a thin stream; beat on high speed about 10 minutes or until mixture is thick.
Makes 2½ cups

lemon glaze

This glaze is used when you want that soft dreamy opaque look on a cake. Use any strained fruit juice you like in place of the lemon juice–be aware that the glaze will take on the color of the juice–or just use water instead. The glaze needs to be poured and spread quickly while it is warm because it begins to set as soon as it starts to cool.

1 cup powdered sugar
1 tablespoon lemon juice, approximately

1 Sift sugar into small heatproof bowl; stir in enough strained juice to give a thick pouring consistency.
2 Stir icing mixture over small saucepan of simmering water until thin enough to make an opaque glaze.
Makes ½ cup

fluffy mock cream

This frosting is whiter, lighter and fluffier than butter cream, and colors better, too. Use any extract or oil you like to flavor the frosting.

2 tablespoons milk
⅓ cup water
1 cup superfine sugar
1 teaspoon gelatin
2 tablespoons water, extra
2 sticks butter, softened
½ teaspoon vanilla extract

1 Combine milk, the water and sugar in small saucepan; stir over low heat, without boiling, until sugar is dissolved. Sprinkle gelatin over extra water in cup, add to pan; stir syrup until gelatin is dissolved. Cool to room temperature.
2 Beat butter and extract in small bowl with electric mixer, until as white as possible. While motor is running, gradually pour in cold syrup; beat until light and fluffy. Mixture will thicken on standing.
Makes 2 cups

dairy-free chocolate frosting

This frosting is easy to handle, rich and luscious, and perfect for people who can't tolerate dairy products. It's a good substitute for ganache.

3 tablespoons dairy-free spread
2 tablespoons water
¼ cup superfine sugar
¾ cup powdered sugar
2 tablespoons cocoa powder

1 Combine spread, the water and superfine sugar in small saucepan; stir over low heat until sugar dissolves.
2 Combine sifted powdered sugar and cocoa in medium bowl; gradually stir in hot spread mixture until smooth. Cover; refrigerate 20 minutes. Using wooden spoon, beat frosting until spreadable.
Makes ¾ cup

ready-made fondant

This icing is available from cake decorating suppliers and craft stores in various colors and flavors, including chocolate. Knead the icing on a surface lightly dusted with powdered sugar until it loses its stickiness. Roll the icing out to the required thickness with a rolling pin on a surface lightly dusted with powdered sugar, or roll between sheets of parchment paper. Keep any icing you're not working with completely airtight by wrapping in foil or plastic wrap. Ready-made icing can be used for covering the tops of cakes, for molding, or for cutting out various shapes, which will dry out at room temperature and hold their shape. You'll be surprised how easy it is to work with; it colors perfectly and the finish looks professional.

decorations

Simple, witty, unique—it's the decoration that transforms a frosted cupcake into a show stopper. We used chocolates and candies in all shapes and sizes, sugared flowers, candles, patterned powder and colored paper cases, to create our individual little cakes.

1 Sugared almonds	**13** Candy Corn	**25** Sugar carrots
2 Mini mints	**14** Strawberry Sour Strap	**26** Various shaped cutters
3 Pastilles	**15** Soft fruit sticks	**27** Gem strings
4 Jujubes	**16** Pearl candies	**28** Peanut brittle
5 Jelly fruit slices	**17** Wedding cakes candles	**29** Sugar booties
6 Small candied pillows	**18** Dried rose buds	**30** Jelly buttons
7 Standard paper cases	**19** Jelly worms	**31** Spearmint leaves
8 Red lip jellies	**20** Cappuccino stencils	**32** Bananas
9 Lifesavers	**21** Tic Tacs	**33** Licorice Cream Rock logs
10 Skittles	**22** Yellow writing icing	**34** Licorice Strap
11 Small jelly beans	**23** Maraschino cherries	**35** Licorice Allsorts
12 SweeTarts	**24** Various sugar flowers	**36** Various sprinkles, dragées & sugar shapes

37 Iced chocolate truffles
38 Ferrero Roche white chocolate truffles
39 Sixlets
40 Cake sparkles
41 Edible glitter
42 Mint Chocolate Drops
43 Malt balls
44 Mini M&M's
45 Eskimo Snowball
46 Raspberry & vanilla marshmallows
47 Chocolate Kisses
48 Various chocolate-coated coffee beans
49 Smarties
50 Junior Mints
51 Rainbow Chips
52 Mini marshmallows
53 Toasted coconut marshmallows
54 Heart chocolates (foil wrapped)
55 Chocolate stars
56 Chocolate shoes
57 Mint Pattie
58 White & dark chocolate chips
59 White & dark chocolate melts
60 Chick-O-Stick
61 Chocolate easter eggs
62 Chocolate mint sticks
63 Lindt chocolate squares
64 Chocolate nonpareils

glossary

almond meal also called ground almonds.

baking powder, gluten-free used as a leavening agent in bread, cake, pastry or pudding mixtures. Suitable for people with an allergic reaction to glutens or seeking an alternative to everyday baking powder.

baking soda also called bicarbonate of soda.

butter use salted or unsalted (sweet) butter.

buttermilk originally the term given to the slightly sour liquid left after butter was churned from cream, today it is commercially made similarly to yogurt. Sold alongside fresh milk products in supermarkets. Despite the implication, it is low in fat.

chocolate

  bittersweet made of cocoa liquor, cocoa butter and sugar.

  melts small disks of compounded dark, milk and white chocolate ideal for melting and molding.

  milk most popular chocolate, mild and very sweet; similar in makeup to dark, but with the addition of milk solids.

  white contains no cocoa solids but derives its sweet flavor from cocoa butter. Very sensitive to heat.

cocoa powder also known as unsweetened cocoa.

coconut

  desiccated concentrated, dried, unsweetened and finely shredded coconut flesh.

  shredded unsweetened thin strips of dried coconut flesh.

  toasted flaked dried flaked coconut flesh, already toasted. Available from health food stores.

corn starch available made from corn or wheat.

eggs we use large chicken eggs weighing 2 ounces. If recipes call for raw or barely cooked eggs, exercise caution if there is a salmonella problem in your area, particularly for children and pregnant women.

flour

  all-purpose also known as plain.

  self-rising all-purpose or whole wheat flour with baking powder and salt added; can be made at home by sifting flour with baking powder in the proportion of 1 cup flour to 2 teaspoons baking powder.

food coloring vegetable-based substance available in liquid, paste or gel form.

gelatin a thickening agent. We used powdered gelatin; also available in sheets known as leaf gelatin.

golden syrup a by-product of refined sugarcane; pure maple syrup or honey can be substituted.

hazelnut meal is made by grinding the hazelnuts to a coarse flour texture.

macadamias fairly large, slightly soft, buttery rich nut. Should always be stored in the refrigerator to prevent their high oil content turning them rancid.

milk we use full-cream homogenized milk unless stated otherwise.

mixed dried fruit a combination of black and golden raisins, currants, mixed citrus peel and cherries.

peppermint oil from the peppermint plant; often used as a flavoring.

pie spice a classic mixture generally containing allspice, nutmeg, ginger and cinnamon; other spices can be added.

polenta also called cornmeal; a flour-like cereal made of dried corn (maize); also the name of the dish made from it.

poppy seeds small, dried, bluish-gray seeds of the poppy plant with a crunchy texture and a nutty flavor. Available whole or ground in most supermarkets and delicatessens.

ready-made fondant prepared rollable firm icing; available in craft shops.

sugar

brown a very soft, fine granulated sugar retaining molasses for its characteristic color and flavor.

powdered also known as confectioners' sugar or icing sugar; pulverized granulated sugar crushed together with a small amount of corn starch.

superfine also known as caster sugar or finely granulated table sugar.

vanilla extract obtained from vanilla beans infused in alcohol.

vegetable oil a number of oils sourced from plant rather than animal fats.

index

conversion chart

measures

All cup and spoon measurements are level. The most accurate way to measure dry ingredients is to use a spoon to fill the measuring cup, without packing or scooping with the cup, and leveling off the top with a straight edge.

When measuring liquids, use a clear glass or plastic liquid measuring cup with markings on the side.

ingredients

Unless otherwise indicated in the recipe, always work with room temperature ingredients. Cold liquids added to butter can cause batters and icings to break.

We use large eggs averaging 2 ounces each. Do not substitute extra large, as the higher amount of protein and volume of the whites can make baked goods tough.

dry measures

METRIC	IMPERIAL
15g	½oz
30g	1oz
60g	2oz
90g	3oz
125g	4oz (¼lb)
155g	5oz
185g	6oz
220g	7oz
250g	8oz (½lb)
280g	9oz
315g	10oz
345g	11oz
375g	12oz (¾lb)
410g	13oz
440g	14oz
470g	15oz
500g	16oz (1lb)
750g	24oz (1½lb)
1kg	32oz (2lb)

liquid measures

METRIC	IMPERIAL
30ml	1 fluid oz
60ml	2 fluid oz
100ml	3 fluid oz
125ml	4 fluid oz
150ml	5 fluid oz (¼ pint/1 gill)
190ml	6 fluid oz
250ml	8 fluid oz
300ml	10 fluid oz (½ pint)
500ml	16 fluid oz
600ml	20 fluid oz (1 pint)
1000ml (1 liter)	1¾ pints

length measures

3mm	⅛in
6mm	¼in
1cm	½in
2cm	¾in
2.5cm	1in
5cm	2in
6cm	2½in
8cm	3in
10cm	4in
13cm	5in
15cm	6in
18cm	7in
20cm	8in
23cm	9in
25cm	10in
28cm	11in
30cm	12in (1ft)

oven temperatures

These oven temperatures are only a guide for conventional ovens. For fan-forced ovens, check the manufacturer's manual.

	°C (CELSIUS)	°F (FAHRENHEIT)	GAS MARK
Very slow	120	250	½
Slow	150	275–300	1-2
Moderately slow	160	325	3
Moderate	180	350–375	4–5
Moderately hot	200	400	6
Hot	220	425-450	7-8
Very hot	240	475	9

DELISH

Elizabeth Shepard   Executive Director

This title was previously published as *Easy Cupcakes by Colour* by ACP books, Sydney Australia

Revised book design by LightSpeed Publishing, Inc., Ashland, Oregon

Photographer   Stuart Scott
Stylist   Vicki Liley
Cake preparation/decoration   Nicole Jennings

Library of Congress Cataloging-in-Publication Data Available Upon Request

10 9 8 7 6 5 4 3 2 1

Published by Hearst Books
A division of Sterling Publishing Co., Inc.
387 Park Avenue South, New York, NY 10016

Delish is a registered trademark of Hearst Communications, Inc.

www.delish.com

For information about custom editions, special sales, premium and corporate purchases, please contact Sterling Special Sales Department at 800-805-5489 or specialsales@sterlingpublishing.com.

Distributed in Canada by Sterling Publishing
c/o Canadian Manda Group, 165 Dufferin Street
Toronto, Ontario, Canada M6K 3H6

Manufactured in China

Sterling ISBN 978-1-58816-934-1